I0158569

Abstract Reality

Written by: Scott Thomas Meyers

Abstract Reality by Scott Thomas Meyers © Copyright 2012. All rights reserved. No part of this book may be reproduced or transmitted in any form or by any means, electronic or mechanical, including photocopying, recording, or by information storage and retrieval systems or other electronic or mechanical methods, without written permission of the Author with exceptions as to brief quotes, references, articles, reviews and certain other noncommercial uses permitted by copyright law. For permission requests, write to the publisher, addressed: "Attention: Permissions," at the address below.

true_beginnings_publishing@yahoo.com

Cover Design, Artwork, and Interior Graphics, Editing and Formatting by True Beginnings Publishing. To contact the publisher, please write to the address, above.

All Illustrations, Cover Art, and Text are Copyright Protected by My Original Works Reference #54514.

Ordering Information:
To order additional copies of this book, please visit Amazon, or:
https://www.createspace.com/4514055

ISBN-13: 978-0615917115
ISBN-10: 0615917119

PRINTED IN THE UNITED STATES OF AMERICA

~Dedication~

I would like to dedicate my first book to my children whom I love and hold dear to my heart. I also would like to thank my friends who have seen me through the light and darkness as I continue to journey on this path which we call life.

I would like to add a special dedication to Bathsheba Dailey and Selina Ahnert for helping me realize my dream. Without their steadfast devotion, these dreams may have never been realized.

Table of Contents

Abstract Reality

The morning sun rises with all its grandeur.
Breaking over the mountains peaks
Its brilliant rays flood the sleepy valley
Covered in the cool damp fog below

With instruments in his shaky trembling hands
The artist scrupulously envisions his masterpiece
To be painted is a theoretical portrait
Of the devastated reflections he sees in his mind's eye

Carefully with brush in hand he paints
Seemingly his image to be portrayed
Fine lines come into view
With anticipation a smile appears upon his face

However with each stroke of the artists hand
The depth and depravity of the pain undauntedly appear
Each stroke becomes much broader than the one before
Beauty now reveals the true nature that of the beast

Scott Thomas Meyers

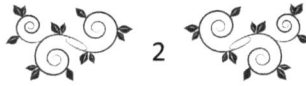

A relentless fight ensues between Doctor Jekyll and Mr. Hyde
The beasts and the demons that torture him
The twisted form of the man he once was
Plagued by the brokenness he so fanatically tries to hide

Thin lines now become blurred
As the colors flow into each other
The merging of two separate images
Are ghastly becoming one

Dutifully the artists meticulously continues his vocation
A new vision has emerged upon his canvass
No longer hiding behind the mask of normality
The abstract of his reality now on display in full view

Peer into the depth of this intangible portrait
Look deeply the truth you will plainly see
The whole of who he is
Vision of his abstract reality

Abstract Reality

Reflections

Images splintered couldn't be clearer

Polished similes - who I truly am

These reflections through a shattered mirror

Abandoning the masks hindering them

Raw emotions void of binding constraints

Mirrored broken shards each a part of me

The self-portrait the mirror always paints

Beauty from depths within - approval free

Cast adorning costumes to the cold gale

Echoes of loneliness, heartache, and pain!

Scott Thomas Meyers

A wake for personal viewing - exhale!

Imprisoned truths no longer to restrain

No longer chained to societal views

Sharing liberty from sorrow and sting

Freedom of expression the path I choose

These reflections the music my heart sings

Cerise tears spill free from this pallid face

Cracked splinters release this confining space!

Fade to Black

Tides ever drifting back towards the sea

Desolation's fog waif upon the shore

Silence critiques giving the third degree

A thousand needles of pain prick each pore

Light absconding as all shades fade to black

Crimson full moon all hope lost before dawn

The demon solitude - keenly attacks

Pureness of love now lays a bleeding swan

Foolish dreams become rains of confusion

Drenched to the bone there aint no coming back

Alone this dream is a mere illusion…

Scott Thomas Meyers

All that's remaining is a granite plaque!

Every truth an empty whitewashed tomb

In the darkness the fire of silence stings

The poison of isolation is my impending doom

Distorting time as the heavy pendulum swings

The catacombs a maze - a one way track

Fearing all is lost when it fades to black!

Blood of Black Ink

Deep within the empty twisted bowels

The poets' words are birthed

Phantasmagorias that are scorched into the mind

The lyrical phrases methodically are formed

A story screaming out so as to be heard

Burns within depths of thy very mortality

Words so often misunderstood

Are the words that pour from thy soul?

The empty white canvass patiently waits

The artist takes pen in hand

Expressive raw emotions

Flow painfully with each drop of ink

Scott Thomas Meyers

A picture to be painstakingly painted

From the very depth of thy soul

Simply a self portrait

It's a story that has to be told

Music beautiful and masterfully orchestrated

Are the words stricken from the hearts chords?

Words of love, sorrow, joy, healing, and pain

One divine purpose to touch others souls

It is a beautiful gift and a heavy affliction

The poets' soul forever on exhibition

For the whole world to see

As he bleeds the blood of black ink

Abstract Reality

No Longer Living in Shades of Gray

There are times to say goodbye

Goodbye to yesterday

The shattered reflections

The fears she held ever so tightly

With dawning of the early light

The glistening droplets of dew

Laying so tenderly upon the ground

With the breaking of dawn - new day has come

One dream faded no longer jaded

That expedition ended long ago

Behind the masks I found who I truly am

Now a new Journey has begun

Scott Thomas Meyers

Taking this life by the reigns

Holding on with all my might

Going to ride this ride

Like it's the last 8 seconds of my life

Living outside the proverbial box

Threw a lit match to the past

It's the step I have to take

May be the longest stride of my life

Like a rocket heading to the stars

I am living for today

Dreaming of vibrant tomorrow

Exploring the realms of outer space

Damn the reruns in the twilight zone

No longer living in shades of gray

Nothing standing in my way

Every second counts when the colors are so bright!

Abstract Reality

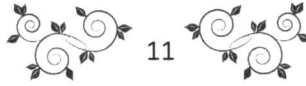

The Stars Don't Shine

Night once again has robbed the light of day

Bitter cold in the dead of night

Even though its 90 degrees

Memories of a brighter time

Haunted continually by the faces I see

Tormented nightly by the lack of sleep

Disheveled – pillows and blankets thrown everywhere

Whisper to me – whisper that it was all a dream

No matter how hard I try

These penned words just don't define

The feelings of emptiness deep inside

In the dead of night where the stars don't shine

The moon she summons me

As If I am her loyal companion

Eerily she forever calls out my name

Scott Thomas Meyers

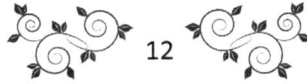

My head hung in shame I have become chained

I have become a slave to the night

I answer her beckon call

Lost forever in the obscurity of the night

Drowning alone in this darkness

No matter how hard I try

These penned words just don't define

The feelings of emptiness deep inside

In the dead of night where the stars don't shine

Wounded I am Bleeding deep on the inside

Crying tears you will never see

Pouring my heart and soul out with my words

Praying one day I will be set free

Free to see the light of day

Where once again the sun will shine

Abstract Reality

My Heart is an Enigma

Confused by darkness and shadows I see

Walls so coldly unsympathetic

Locked deeply inside I'll never be free

Smiles and laughter their all merely cosmetic

River of tears dried up ages ago

Tell me who the hell I am supposed to be

The wounds you inflected were a mortal blow

Always and forever has become my hell for eternity

Darkness has chased away the light of day

Tormenting me are the demons in my mind

A creature of the night I keep everyone at bay

Hauntingly these scales keep my hearts eye blind

Scott Thomas Meyers

This journey to be traveled alone

The thickets draw blood in the blackness

Through the wildness my soulless body roams

As my flesh becomes the razors canvas

Tears of blood have strewn my face

In despair and anguish I cry to be free

To love and be loved my desires retrace

My heart is an enigma even to me.

Abstract Reality

Upon Scarlet Winds

Shall love be found eternally weeping?

Like the willow her branches bowed down

Somberly broken her hope ever sleeping

Is true love nothing more than a passive noun?

Upon scarlet winds hearts forever reach

Restless nights pleading for elusive dawns

Stitched lips prayerful for freedom of speech

As verses rest quietly like serene swans

Begging for faith to take upon wings and soar

Once again through crimson fields and frigid air

Settling for nothing less - searching nothing more

Then to find her true love - her soul's only prayer

Passions scorch from the infernos of her heart

From this solemn flight - never shall she depart

Scott Thomas Meyers

Whispers

A tender caress and loving touch

Feelings so surreal still burning today

Dreams and visions that meant so much

Romance played out like a romantic play

A sweet loving forbidden embrace

Kisses so tender yet ever so deep

Recalling the smile upon your face

Whispers locked away ours to keep

Whispering can true love really be wrong

Sweet first kisses that left us breathless

Our hearts danced joyful to a new song

Inferno's of passion that rendered us helpless

Raw emotions burned as words were spoken

Whispers now leaving hearts splintered and broken

Abstract Reality

Alone

Words so very hard to speak

Emotions flow from the hidden abyss

A heart too heavy to bear

As I cry these invisible tears

Vivid Memories played like an old movie

Colors and lines how they become blurred

Once vivid brilliant vibrant colors

Now just shades of blacks and grays

Walking in the darkness of the night

Hiding myself from the light of day

So hard to be sure when

But death occurred a long time ago

Scott Thomas Meyers

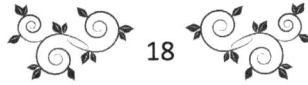

Like an eerie ghostly figure

Trapped within these four walls

Cursed to relive this torturous death

I wandered the infernal past

Love is so distant and obscure

When a heart is splintered and damaged

Words so eloquently spoken

Yet I feel so broken and insecure

Doomed to forever roam

Imprisoned unmercifully inside myself

I call out in the dead of perpetual night

Finding myself eternally alone

Alone in this dreadful darkness

Lost in a pool of empty emotions

Nomadic I drift through my plight

I've become invisible and isolated

Abstract Reality

Shrouded in the darkness

Feeling as I have become no more

Loneliness is an abysmal identity

This place I no longer desire to be!

I simply must say goodbye

It's no longer a life mystery

All that I am or ever was

Is just simply better left unsaid!

Scott Thomas Meyers

Oh What a Tangled Web is Weaved

Oh what a tangled web is weaved

When in our hearts we live in doubts believed.

Is it so hard to speak and believe in the truth?

We long for the love we dreamed of as youth.

Loneliness is such a hard path to escape.

When behind walls our hearts have been raped.

Accustomed to the darkness of the midnight hours,

We dare to dream from our prison towers.

Thoughts racing endlessly through our mind,

Searching for the sanity that we can't seem to find!

Keys for our freedom jingle at the cell door.

Cowering in the dark on the dampness of the floor!

Oh what a tangled web is weaved

When in our hearts we live in doubts believed.

Abstract Reality

I Can't Write This Story

I can't pen those lovely words

That will make one heart flutter

Visions of passion, romance, and love

There is simply is not enough time to say

Lying here mortally wounded

Drowning in my tears of blood

My fortress - a pool of shattered dreams

Walls built – impenetrable they stand

Learning to hide in my shallow grave

The truth needs to be forever written

Inscribed upon the canvass of my heart

This dreadful pain will never grow old

Scott Thomas Meyers

Scribbling for all I am worth

I can't write the ending of this story

Even with all my poetic words

My pen just simply isn't that good

Words escape my heart - yet -

No audible sound flows from my lips

With pen in hand I picture a love so true

However the ink dried up ages ago

Take a look at my face

See through my dark empty eyes

Fearing I died on the inside

All that's left are river of tears I cried

Abstract Reality

Tell me how love is truthfully meant to be

A fairytale like we all dreamed

Romeo and Juliet paint a convincing picture

Of a love went awry - another tragic play

Truth is there is no price I wouldn't pay

To have and hold - this emotion called love

A forever if there is such a thing

Two halves wholly made complete

Always and forever words beautifully spoken

Forever just seems to end another day

Always hoping for those magical words to rhyme

My pen awaits this story to be written in sands of time!

Scott Thomas Meyers

Hourglass Moments

Are dreams to descend into the Dead Sea?

Shall passion and desire be left a mere tease?

Oh my heart shall darkness fall upon thee?

Will dawn find me broken dropped to my knees?

Shall the sunrise break in all her glory?

Refreshing life with her droplets of dew

Shall black ink fill pages with a new story?

Only hopes light will tell the tale anew

Shall the pen's serene quill romance her heart?

Whispers from the soul beseeching for this

Shall hearts ablaze create new works of art?

Painting masterpieces with just her kiss

Shall time forever stand silently still?

Hourglass moments watching every grain spill!

Abstract Reality

Harmonious Love Shall Forever Sing

Shall whispers fall silent from lover's lips?

Kisses left void under the moons soft glow

Shall two hearts be hid in total eclipse?

Love's embrace die under the winter's snow

Shall passion's flame be quenched by fallen rain?

Caresses left untouched upon naked skin

Shall music fall hushed on empty refrains?

Songbirds muted beg release from within

Once true loves arrow penetrates the heart

Treble clefs and half notes assigned wings fly

Symphonic scores hungering to impart

Affections notes float through the cobalt sky

Harmonious love shall forever sing

When elegantly strummed from the hearts string!

Scott Thomas Meyers

Chained By This Melodic Gravity

Words so perfectly and skillfully melded together

Longing feeds this refining fire of desire

Verses delicately fallen beseeching of a forever

Sweat raptures life – two rhythmical hearts do aspire

Field of dreams floating upon the eastern gales

Secret gardens lay within the Labyrinth of my heart

Words painting imagery to which creation pales

Lost within this arena of dreams – never wishing to part!

Melody of words provoking the heart to sing

Soulfully pouring out lyrics – with pen and ink

Majestically trapped within this musical poetic fling

Chained by this melodic gravity an unbreakable link

All I can savor is the beauty of these expressions

Forever scribed in the tempests of my mind,

Harmonious beauty leaving indelible impressions

This is the true glory to which my heart is assigned!

Abstract Reality

I Dream of You

Two ships tossed helplessly in the darkness of the night

Longing to find solace in the midst of their plight

The truth behind the journey from their very start

Has been nothing less than to find a kindred heart

Along this lonely course alone they have traveled

Hoping to restore the dreams that were unraveled

In the midst of the chaos and the storm

Souls are hopefully refreshed - to this their heart does warm

Longing to dry up the river of tears

Desiring to calm the storms and ease all fears

In The darkness alone and awake

Heartfelt emotions - are surreal make no mistake

The smile upon your lovely face

My fingers with anticipation they long to trace

When I close my eyes this much is true

Every time I dream - I dream of you!

Scott Thomas Meyers

Before The Dawn

Through the gates of hell I enter

The flames eternally licking at my flesh

The stench of failure burns my nose

Scorched my soul can bear no more

The blackness of the night

Engulfs me in this endless nightmare

Though sleep escapes me

Shaken myself to be awake on the inside

Screaming for a departure from the darkness

From the nothingness I now have become

Where is the light I now so desperately crave?

Shall I be sewn into the folds of the darkness?

Even the stars have hidden themselves from me

Fearing I will be lost forever drifting aimlessly

Drifting forever lost upon the empty horizon

Far away from Gods celestial shore

Shake me! Wake me up!

Call my name lest I be lost forever

It's all ways darkest before the dawn

Remember - it's always darkest before the dawn!

Scott Thomas Meyers

Wherefore Art Thou

This question continually plagues my mind

Visions of thee haunt my dreams

Though the darkness would have me be blind

I imagine you with perfect clarity so it seems

My beloved - Wherefore Art Thou?

Why have thy kept me waiting for so long

This heartache weighs heavy upon my brow

Must it be that true love time doth prolong

How is it that my mind doth picture this so clear?

Unconditional love and a romance so pure

Thy absence makes me tremble in fear

This love I so desire – this essence I have to procure

In my eyes, thy beauty, poise, and grace I do see

The fair maiden that captivates my soul

Her face etched forever - how can this be?

Abstract Reality

Yet the absence of this heart has left massive hole

How did it to come be my beloved

That this passion burns within my heart?

A dream unbending, never ending, yet a heart unloved

Explain to me why our kindred spirits are apart?

My beloved I have to know thee.

Passionate desires to feel your touch

To love you wholly and completely this I decree!

The irony of this dream is just too much

I can feel your lips as they tenderly kiss me

Your skin soft and tender like petals of a rose

Your eyes summon my heart to thee

All this beauty - how is this do you suppose.

My Enchantress my heart bleeds crimson red

My beloved - Wherefore art thou?

My temptress - wipe away all the tears that I have shed

Wherefore art thou – Wherefore art thou?

Scott Thomas Meyers

This Empty House

This empty house

A place I called home

Dreams of a forever

Forever never to be known

If these walls could tell a story

It would be of the tears I have cried

A prisoner of my own doing

Locked away hiding in the ruins

Hidden behind the cold damp walls

Are the haunted visions

Visions and dreams of you

I became a captive within these walls!

Abstract Reality

Chained and bound in the darkness

A tortured wretched soul I became

Aimlessly wandering our past

This house we called home

Will hold me no more

Freedom has always waited

Just outside the front door

The shackles have fallen

Fallen to the damp prison floor

Your ghostly spirit will have to walk alone

As I bid farewell to this empty house

A place that I once called my home!

Scott Thomas Meyers

The Strength He Chooses to Portray

You see a smile on his worn face

The twinkle in his hazel eyes

Masking the brokenness he feels

The strength he chooses to portray

The years liberally have taken their toll

The night brings her furry and terror

Daybreak he once again hides his pain

He looks at the horizon with drifting eyes

Screaming in the silence of the night

So that no one will hear his hearts cry

Holding on by one lonely thread

His mind wanders as he longs to be free!

Abstract Reality

Gazing intently he looks into the mirror

Afraid of the truths others might see

Forcing the smiles upon his face

He wanders lost throughout the day!

Shattered reflections of who he once was

Haunted by the ghostly images of the past

Lost in the obscurity of hollow tomorrows

Striving once more for strength to portray!

Scott Thomas Meyers

Destiny

Shadows within the dark of night

Mystery clouds the sunny day

Inside my fortress a mere reflection

Images of the man I thought I once was

Drowning in my tears of blood

Shame the remnants of broken dreams

Shattered images and self-reflections

The totality of who I am

With pen in hand I carve at my own heart

Hungrily longing with insatiable desire

Choosing all that I am or will ever be

With apparent abandonment of all sanity

Enchantments entice the essence of my soul

Unfulfilled dreams that are meant to be

The passion that feverishly burns

Giving myself over to this voracious desire

Driven by my visions and my dreams

Like a butterfly - hope floats effortlessly

The wind beneath me - soaring high and free

This is my desire - this is my destiny!

Scott Thomas Meyers

The Flaming Eternal Rose

What words penned can speak of loves legacy

Shall memoirs become pale as time grows old?

Scented imagery inspires ecstasy

Breathtaking colors as petals unfold

Thirsting for rain - budding in the desert

Leaves turn to dust as weather changes

Time lazily fades as seasons convert

Soulful essence spills black ink on blank pages

Joyful memoirs the hearts hidden treasure

No manner of love shall ever grow old

Intimacy and friendship pure pleasure

Cracks in pavement birthing seedlings foretold

Love's memories a true concerto to compose

Paying tribute to loves flaming eternal rose!

Abstract Reality

You Are My Muse - I Am Your Clay

Making those midnight promises

Pictures elaborately painted in my mind

Images gracefully effortlessly dancing

Like an elegant ballerina on her final day

Tender delicately spoken words

Sweeter than the purest honey

Flow like a swollen river

Washing over this heart of red clay

Visions of opulence clear my cloudy skies

Dreams of a love that bountifully overflows

My heart an empty parched vessel

Waiting to filled with that new red wine

You are my muse - I am your clay

Creations longing for their birth,

Scott Thomas Meyers

There's a story yet to be written

Our destiny the beginning of the play

Tired of being that lost soul out of place

Even the coldest winter's ice melts away

Rose buds forcefully push to the nourishing light

Waiting for that glory that last a whole life through

Deaths grip no choice but to yield to new life

Shattered hearts mending with hopes of new love

Time has a way of making everything new

Loss gives birth to a dream of a forever through and through!

Abstract Reality

Here in this Grassy Meadow

The cool wind is blowing

Within this plush grassy meadow

Arms out stretched eyes tightly closed

With an open heart I am standing still

The wind consoles me

As she wraps herself around me

The sun swept rays ever warming

As they tenderly break through the leaves

Serenity likened to the graceful lily

Poised gallantly in the valley

Unscathed by the onslaught of humanity

Peace from the depths of my soul fills me

Scott Thomas Meyers

The old man on the mountain speaking

From the tips of his snow-capped peaks

To valley that lay beneath his feet

Words flowing like a river overflowing

A new fresh gentle breeze blows

Releasing my once besieged spirit

A vision even the blinded eye can see

Atlas my spirit will soar - peacefully free

Beauty beyond intellectual capacity

Here in this grassy meadow

All that ever was or will ever be

I simply am - finally just me!

Abstract Reality

No Longer Blinded by Life's Delusions

Leaves rustling dead on the ground

Upon the currents of the fall wind

Whispers in the dead of night

Forever she is calling my name

Spellbound by sweet enticing rapture

This journey is not for the faint of heart

Likely more than not it's left to the insane

As a simple gypsy moth is drawn to the flame

Seduced by the flickering images

The hunger, longing, and insatiable desire

Passion feverishly burns within this light

Unfulfilled dreams match wanting desires

Scott Thomas Meyers

Shadows linger within the dark of night

Mystery hazes the sunny day

Words sometimes better left unspoken

We are mere mortal men made of clay

This becoming is harder than it seems

Finding myself that I thought long lost

Daring to dream a mere desire to believe

A heartfelt aspiration simply just to be

Scales forcefully removed from my eyes

No longer blinded by delusions

Humbly broken – upon bended knee

Heeding the winds enchanting song!

Abstract Reality

Serendipity

Today I make of you this inquiry

Why must a troubled soul

Paint a portrait for you to behold

An artist picks up his tools

To capture what's in his mind's eye

On display, a creation for all to see

Peer deeply into thy wounds

Your interpretation, the breath of life

Each masterpiece painstakingly created

Every stroke a touch of the master's hand

Stand there gazing and peering deeply into thy soul

The palate of colors wisely chosen by the artist

Scott Thomas Meyers

The colors and images pour from the depth of thy fiber

With each stroke of the artists brush

Escapes the heartache - my words from my soul!

On display for all to see, I now find myself the muse.

From artist to muse how the tables have now turned

From words which were born from the depths within

I find myself on display for the world to watch

Gaze in to the depths of my heart and the words that I write

A two way mirror for the entire world to see

What a reflection you see when looking at me

You see yourself in the portrait of words that I paint

On display are heartache loneliness and strife

Abstract Reality

Nay not only that ~ but a heart that is pure and true

Hope and assurance in the midst of life's storms

Daring to dream with boldness and in the richest of colors

A discovery of untold treasures!

Lies within each stroke of the masters tool

A creation from a troubled soul

Displayed elegantly and meticulously

This portrait of words for you to behold

Simply call it serendipity!

Scott Thomas Meyers

Sleepless Nights

Restless, wide-awake lost deep in my thoughts

Memoirs assault my heart - they plague my mind

Recalling the demons that I have fought

Through the alchemist fire I am refined

Battles of life and death are they for naught?

What's left of me what will I leave behind?

My legacy constantly my forethought

Counting grains of sand to which I am confined

Tortured - naive I lay here and fight

Twisted and broken with this I must contend

Angel's first sight - pleading to flee to their light

Illness and pain I can no longer pretend

Abstract Reality

Chained in this prison wingless for one last flight

Night's bitter cold and damp when dying in fear

Hopes empty when the reapers sword looms in the night

Deaths expedition my final frontier

Silence moans when cut short from the human race

I lay here awake another sleepless night

With boldness death and life I embrace

The hell with it all - what's one more fight

Time will cease - fighting to survive will come to an end

My poetic words forged forever in your minds

From this earthly realm my soul will transcend

Blood of black ink to forever remind!

Scott Thomas Meyers

Treading Angel Dust

Damn these games of Russian roulette

From dusk to dawn bells ravenously chime

Bravery a mere empty silhouette

Counting grains of sands just to keep time

Surely a dream swimming in the Dead Sea

At hells gates standing on heaven shore

The blinded eyes are truly too dark to see

Reality I don't want to face any more

Fanged appetites thirsting for soul and blood

Between light the shadows they blankly stare

Hope frail as thread while shoveling mud

Scents of your existence lingers in stale air

Divine whispers of dark sinister lust

Lingering in the dusk treading angel dust!

Abstract Reality

Sandcastles in Heaven

In Memory of Maci Lynn Emery 2010 – 2012

Knowing we needed an angel to guide

God searched throughout the kingdom of heaven

Past the streets of gold - by the crystal sea

He found Maci Lynn playing in the sand

It is with tearful eyes we remember

Your heaven sent angelic reflections

Innocent sparkles that kindled your eyes

Your laughter - the flame to our hearts ember

A mother's love that heard your midnight cries

Your arms outstretched were a grandmother's praise!

Scott Thomas Meyers

Playfulness your family's recollections

For us that loved you - a wonderful prize

You've completed your heaven sent mission

In your blue eyes we saw God's reflection

Returning to God the Father above

You resume your playful disposition

When we see the sandcastles in heaven

We will find Maci playing in the sand!

Abstract Reality

Blood Stained Sand

Clay mortars busting with celebration

Lifting eyes to the star spangled sky

A glimpse of a proud united nation

Grieving widows and children begging why

Colors amusingly paint the black night

The sounds of freedom ringing through and through

Rejoicing we stand in awe of the light

Mouths agape waiting the finale's cue

Scenery contrasting from land to land

The clay mortars burst with anger and wrath

Only red paints the heated desert sand

A 3-volley salute the aftermath

Freedoms price - a high cost for this or any land

Liberties high tax always found in blood stained sand!

Scott Thomas Meyers

Hells Angelic Rose

In the ash of failed burnt sacrifices

Lay a broken embellished granite alter

Beset by the rubble that lay before me

Chained by tuneful songs of melancholy

Solace in the dark hours of solitude

Was this fate and all else merely a dream

To reign over vast voids of nothingness

Shattered imaginings never meant to be

Black ink spilled tells the never-ending story

The demons clawing - scarring flesh and psyche

Endless battles - victories incomplete

N0! - From hells fallow silt sewn earth - hope abounds!

Abstract Reality

Shimmering light piercing the darkest of nights

Seedlings of hope and love begin to sprout

Hair as red as the crimson lakes of fire

Eyes hypnotic blue as heavens crystal seas

Against all odds hells angelic rose unfolds

Her angelic wings tightly wrap around

Drawing me this enchantress sings her song

Chained to her heart - forever I am bound

Scott Thomas Meyers

Everything Is Meant to be Broken

Hiding behind walls thick and cold

Tears crystallized upon pale white cheeks

Forever stained are hearts painted crimson red

Breathing in the damp coolness of loneliness

Hiding I don't think they will understand me

Words softly spoken from the lips of dread

When everything is meant to be broken

When did we believe and breathe in life

The moment that everything felt so right

Hope floating like butterflies in the sky

So effortlessly hearts blissfully dream

Daring to forever believe

Abstract Reality

57

Everything is meant to be broken

As the day gives way to the darkness

Shadows devour the flame of life

And the death of darkness takes its toll

A voice in the darkness calling out your name

Across the chasm dreams fly

Everything is meant to be broken

Even the heavy iron chains that bind

Cold links falling to the damp concrete floor

Loudly clanking are the keys to your cell

No needing to give up forever

Everything is meant to be broken

Scott Thomas Meyers

Lift up your head and to the heavens soar

The sun upon your skin will thaw out those tears

Pale skin void of life's precious blood

Heartbeats away from what was once rosy red

Everything is meant to be broken

Even the depth of this loneliness

Savor the moment and the dream

And dare once again to believe!

Stained

Black roses rest upon your grave

Holding you forever in my arms

Broken beside you I forever lay

Crimson stained tears soaking the earth

The raven watches from his perch

Your spirit eternally entwined with mine

Your sleeping soul awaiting its new birth

Breaking free from the chains of your demise

My sleepless ambiance never at rest

Peering through my soulless eyes

Your love imprisons the essence of my being

Igniting a flame from the shadows of your tomb

Scott Thomas Meyers

Meagerly clad mourners carved your granite stone

Angels drape over you in agony and despair

Hour glass with wings - the fleeting passage of time

Inverted torches symbolism of love stolen to soon

The willow tree broken she mourns

As she bends wretchedly toward the earth

The raven incisively pecking from its stone perch

Methodically opens the crimson stained earth

Your spirit so forebodingly cold

Awaits the sustenance of my lively embrace

Breathing life into your immortal being

Opening your eyes to our eternal touch

A love eliminated way before its prime

Passion and desire eternally on fire

Your face meticulously sketched

Stained forever in my mind!

Abstract Reality

My Soul Is Yours to Take

The bell tower eerily looms in the night

Awaiting the darkest of hours

Tick tock - tick tock - the final bell tolls

Time magically stands ever so still

Pending is my apparent fate

The darkest of the midnight hours

This is your kingdom to rule

While you Perch upon your granite throne

The black sinister emissary of death

You watch tolerantly - dejectedly you wait

Screaming in silent my cries are in vain

Fearfully I do my best to hide from you

Scott Thomas Meyers

I must be hallucinating - this simply can't be

That black lacquer box - glistening ever so brightly

Now entombs my lifeless body – shouldn't be shocked

My heart you pilfered long ago

Why must this vision of dread I see

Thinking of all the things I could have said

A war ensues between dark and light

Demons and angels fight for my soul

A spectator I am forced to helplessly watch

Those who will decide my fate

I can't take much more of this watching

Shovel after shovel of dirt, they dig my hole

Is this my only chance of escape

Or is it that I am still trying to hide

Caught up in this game of cat and mouse

I must try to plot a twist of fate

Abstract Reality

Rhetoric pours from my lips

Talking to you like an innocent child

Yet I truly don't know how to feel

All of these emotions plague my mind

Writhing in agony and in pain

Feeling like all I am has been washed away

Trying to do all the right things

Yet I have become numb no longer do I feel

While those who are alive slumber!

I force myself to stay awake

Knowing full well – if I sleep

My soul is yours to take!

Scott Thomas Meyers

The Seclusion of the Open Sea

Night black and dark as coal

Through the unbearable darkness

Of the midnight hour

Silence that was deafening

Through it all I have drifted endlessly

On the seclusion of the open sea

In uncharted waters

The wind unmercifully tossed me

Bound and chained to the mast

In the midst of the furious storms

Thunder crashing in the eastern skies

Lightening crackling in the dead of the night

Abstract Reality

The sails tattered and torn

The splintered mast laying bedsides me

The ship now badly battered

Debris clutters the raging sea

To my knees I have fallen

The angry sea hauntingly she laughs

Proclaiming victory at the sight of my vessel

Tossing me to and fro

Water now floods the hull

My soul trembles as I fear all is lost

Shattered like the splintered mast

These are remnants of broken dreams

Scott Thomas Meyers

Silently I scream

In the dead of the night

Through storms that plague my life

I dare to believe

In the darkness of midnight hour

Though my vessel is battered

The sails weathered and worn

I passionately set my course

With the breaking of the dawn

I have mastered the storm

With tears of liberation

I laugh back at the sea!

Abstract Reality

Listen To the Wind

The wind she whispers my name

With each howl she cries to me

Hiding inside myself

There is no one left to blame

The monsters angrily claw at my skin

They hunger for and devour my flesh

They crave the very essence of my being

As I fight for and cling to every last breathe

Gasping for that precious life

Hiding within these four walls

My so called refuge

The night speaks the actuality as you dream

Scott Thomas Meyers

Your reality is just a delusion

A young man's visions

The remains of old men's dreams

The truth ~ chaos reigns as the demons feed

The moon illuminating the cloudy sky

The bitter cold rain falls

Drowning out all noise

As the nightmare continues

Soaked to the very core

Droplets running down my face

The thunder clashes

As the lightening hits the ground

Lingering in the darkness

Cowering inside myself no more

Fighting back the monsters

I stand from my feeble knees

Abstract Reality

Ripping the door from these rusty hinges

I now feverishly plan my escape

I know what lies beyond these four walls

My reality and your pain

You look at me as if I lost my mind

The truth is that I can admit

What you try to inconspicuously hide

Hiding within yourselves – hiding in fear and pain

This dark dreary midnight hour

In the silence of your echoing chaos

Listen to the wind

She is calling out your name!

Scott Thomas Meyers

The Desert

Through the desolate desert I travel

Parched withered cracked lips beg of intense thirst

Condemned! Lonely the verdict unravels

Fated to the wastelands I'm not the first

Muteness deafens when it's the only sound

Words cannot escape a dry dusty soul

Exiled to the crimson hedgehog I'm bound

No penance my skin becomes black as coal

Words penned laid to rest - the next Dead Sea scroll

Shall this be my fate - faded black ink spilled?

Nay, in Death Valley the thunder clouds roll

Nomadic soul - dreams yet to be fulfilled

Babbling brooks spill the blood of satin ink

This oasis your soul shall ever drink!

Abstract Reality

Enchantress of My Heart

It was thy beauty that captivated my soul

Thy eyes that led my heart astray

Thy lips sweeter then honey took their toll

Your beauty and poise graced my days

The shimmering nights of longing and passion

Unspeakable desire beseeches my heart

Both love and lust for thee my heart did fashion

Beautiful melody of words enchanted me from the start

Enchantress upon bended knee I beseech thee

Let loose of this temptress enchantment of a spell

Lest I shall be lost within thine eyes for eternity

And dragged eternally willing to the depths of hell

Nevertheless if this spell cast shall remain

A love the depth of this - truly has no shame!

Scott Thomas Meyers

The Music Box

Harmonious refrains on silver rolls

Musical notes floating through the blue sky

Plucked tuned teeth of steel combs comforting souls

Half notes and Treble clefs assigned wings fly

Shall music comfort when this box is closed

Sleeping alone upon the mirrored ledge

Poised graceful its gift forever enclosed

Beseeching sweet release – delight its pledge

Nay this box is your crimson bleeding heart

Symphonic scores are longing to unfold

Melodic compositions of pure art

When unrestrained - sings charming songs foretold

Angelic tunes shall forever sing

When elegantly strummed from the hearts strings!

Abstract Reality

My Secret Desire

I've soared with angels high in the heavens

Evoking imagery of love untold

Equated and estimated seconds

Watching in revulsion heartache unfold

Feeling the rush of the mighty whirlwind

Uncertainty can anyone be true

Fragmented proclaiming don't fall again

Falling in love is a hard task to do

Dreaming - beseeching she will come to me

Fervent tried true love my heart doth aspire

Breaking chains setting imprisoned souls free

Love and be loved - my true secret desire

Hearts blossoming like a beautiful rose

Waterfalls cascading of hope renewed

Exquisite symphonies yet to compose

No longer can these visions be subdued!

Scott Thomas Meyers

Dreaming of You

Dreaming of you during the night

Visions of you in the twilight

Longing to wipe away all tears

To calm your storms and ease your fears

Truth and hope my heart doth recite

To be your beaming guiding light

Solace in the midst of your plight

Upon my bow cast all your cares

Dreaming of you

Thoughts of you make my heart ignite

Lovely eyes pierce my soul forthright

Heartfelt laughter a gift that shares

To your sweet smile nothing compares

Two kindred hearts giving to flight

Dreaming of you!

Abstract Reality

The Rivers of Desire

Emotions flow fluidly through my head

Kindly probing my passions deep within

Beauty and longing that I feared long dead

Rivers of desires needing to be fed

Waterfalls cascading from streams once thin

Emotions flow fluidly through my head

Rarity - hanging on words thin as thread

Exploring not knowing where to begin

Beauty and longing that I feared long dead

Scott Thomas Meyers

The river - hope - her icy rocks I tread

Free falling submerged forever therein

Emotions flow fluidly through my head

Rapids of want wash through my riverbed

Treading whirlpools - exciting desires spin

Emotions flow fluidly through my head

Beauty and longing that I feared long dead!

The Very Last Tear

With the falling of the very last tear

Ripples will flower through the sands of time

Song birds shall sing ballads to ease all fear

Upon crystalline seas sorrows made clear

Messages from the heart revealed through rhyme

With the falling of the very last tear

Pallid dreams bleakly floating through the air

Hearts vexing to beat to iambic time

Song birds shall sing ballads to ease all fear

Scott Thomas Meyers

Rhetoric pours out in form of prayer

Invisible box entombed like a mime

With the falling of the very last tear

Through the mirrored looking glass I shall peer

Angelic wings lifting as the bells chime

With the falling of the very last tear

Song birds shall sing ballads to ease all fear!

Insatiable Desire

Drawn in by the luster of your silken spun webs

Captured by the glistening beauty of each woven line

Wrapped within your grasp as cannibalistic lust ebbs

Upon each other's savory flesh we insatiably dine

Blindfolded and tethered by vigorous incarnate desire

Vehement hunger dampens your parched yearning lips

Firm touches pulsating into an uncontainable wildfire

Master and mistress enslavement within zealous grips

Adorned with droplets of fiery beads of sensual sweat

Entangled in your embrace as your body forcefully rolls

Begging for sweet release together we sing our duet

To our carnal desire we pleasurably hand over our souls!

Scott Thomas Meyers

Danse Macabre

The blackness of night and all of her glory

Oh how she falls gracefully so silently

The moon how she breaks above the brow

T'was upon this starry night the angels fell

A coin for payment or for bribe to the ferryman

I must now abide - to cross this elusive divide

Upon this glassy gruesome river I Journey

Upon his decrepit old wooden boat I now ride

A journey so often taken - yet so ill received

Surely a vision for only the blind to see

In the mist, the shadows they blankly stare

Twisting and turning on this river to hell

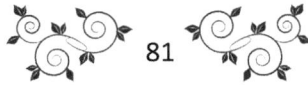

The ritual has begun as the music starts

A melody of your own sinister choosing

Methodically plays as the final bell tolls

Spellbound we meet on the ballroom floor

And we danced - you and I

It was to a felicitous blend of song

Joined in dance - held by deaths own hand

Gripped ensuing your baleful beckon call!

Scott Thomas Meyers

Elemental Desire

Love is purely a rare mixture of elemental desires

An alchemy that burns feverishly out of control

A combining of the natural elements transpires

Let it be a deliciously wicked, unmerciful wildfire

Tantalizing heat freeing itself from the longing soul

Love is purely a rare mixture of elemental desires

Immersed within the oceanic depths to which they aspire

Drowning gracefully in the beauties hidden in the depths below

A combining of the natural elements transpires

Breathing in the air you expel filling the wells of desire

Floating upon the Jasmine scented winds losing self -control

Love is purely a rare mixture of elemental desires

Abstract Reality

Insatiable arousal and gravitational orbits - Oh how they conspire

Salacious seeds of want and desire their flowering gifts they bestow

Where a combining of the natural elements doth transpire

Loves elemental forces two hearts they require

Lost forever in each other's ambiance and radiant glow

Love is purely a rare elemental desire

A combining of the natural elements transpires!

If Love Is To Be the Earth

If love is to be the blessed mother earth

Then it shall be the richest dark fertile soil

Seedlings impregnated with hopes of new birth

Prospering only through blood, tears, and toil

Let love be formed from a solid granite foundation

Upon this rock we shall build our beloved church

Standing purer and truer than any mighty nation

Flowering peacefully like the ambitious white birch

Let the roots of passion delve deep within the ground

Standing gallantly taller than the mighty sequoia tree

Where majestic beauty, peace, and grace can be found

Like the mountains above the fruited plains for all to see

Let it be volcanic eruptions - passionately erupting liquid fire

Or oceanic tides washing with uninhibited unquenchable desire

Abstract Reality

If Love Is To Be the Air

If love is to be the air

The sustenance of life so cherished

Than let me finally just breathe

Taking in this breath of fresh air

If love is to be the air

Then lift me it shall upon on gentle wings

From the gray ashen clay where I now lay

Delivering me from the depths of this shallow grave

If love is to be the air

Then let it harbor the midnight mist

Waking my fearfully lost wandering heart

Under the moons mirrored illuminating light

Scott Thomas Meyers

If love is to be the air

Let it be like the brisk summer breeze

Lavender, chamomile, and jasmine scented

Coolly refreshing my skin on a sweltering day

If love is to be the air

Let it be ravishingly temptingly hot

Dancing across my begging desirous flesh

Windswept – soulfully moving as it erotically plays

If love is to be the air

Then let me gasp for just one last breath...

Abstract Reality

On Bended Knee

If love is to be this magnificent untamed ocean

Let the fullness of its glory wash over my soul

Quenching my thirst with its healing potion

The waves thrashing at my heart as I lose control

Let me dive in to the depths of the deep blue sea

And let me forever bask in the beauties hidden below

To be lost in the richness of this splendor - my only plea

Upon the reflective waters in the moons silvery glow

Oh to be drowning kindly within these vibrant brine's

As they wash wholly over - calming the stormy heart

Baptized in the depths- a new birth with new designs

From these sustaining waters my soul would never part

If love can be compared to the deep blue sea

Then my heart is found wishing for this on bended knee

Scott Thomas Meyers

Loves Fire

If love is to be the transmuting fire

Then verily I say your heart is the spark

Black velvet words of pure intrinsic desire

Inscribed tenderly - eternally leaving their mark

If love is to be the undying flame

Your elegant lyrics are the wick that capture the fire

Burning ravenously to which there is no shame

The beauty of this love my heart does aspire

If love is to be a sizzling blaze

Lost in the glowing hues of its raptures coals

Than dance we shall in the twilight of its rays

As refining fire reclaims our restless souls

If love is to be this immortal fire

Than be engulfed we will within its voracious flame

Baptizing our souls with the glow of passion and desire

Eternally consumed as two lovers become one in the same

Abstract Reality

Lovely Solitude

Back into the damp darkness from whence I came

Cold black eyes piercing the depths of my dark soul

Undone - Never the more shall I remain the same

Catatonic eyes stare into my core

From the grave enchantments strangely loom

How long will it take before blind eyes see?

The abysmal depths - your enticing depravity

Lonely finding myself lost within the depths of you

Methodically the Sirens sing invitingly

Black lovely angelic wings pulling me in

Forgotten completely abandoned

Captivated lost deep within your folds

Angelic whispers of sinister lust

My enchanting temptress in you I abide

Forever beautifully you - forever me

Lost deeply within your lovely solitude

Scott Thomas Meyers

Black Satin Ink

Black satin ink so elegantly and thoughtfully spilled

Inscribed on the crimson canvass that is my heart

Delicately handcrafted - intrinsically skilled

Whispering from the depths escaping the heart

Terms of endearment scribed on a cerise waxy scroll

Golden keys of fiery passion jingle at the frozen doors

Poetic harmonious melodies – loves virtues they extol

Seething from the essence of life – escaping thy pores

Verses resting upon angelic wings – taking on their flight

Rising from the broken shards and the lifeless vestiges

Upon the gentle winds soaring in the darkness of night

Beautiful dreams lay within these melodic messages

The keys lay within this gracefully spilled black satin ink

Written on the canvass of my heart taking me to the brink

Abstract Reality

Tears Red as Blood

Tears free falling shadowy red as Blood

From a heart that's been mortally wounded

Crimson tears wash over my soul like a flood

Love that has been shunned - a voice now muted

Rose peddles falling to the ground turning to dust

Forever entombed in darkness chained in disgrace

From a heart that was once vibrant and robust

Sealed away an eternity from the human race

A heart in the wasteland - longing to be set free

This poetic realm is a dark abysmal foreboding place

Crying out save me! Can anyone hear my plea

Loneliness bathes my soul as pale washes over my face

Will I be consumed by the waters of this raging flood?

As they wash-down me - these crimson tears of blood

Dreams beneath Icy Waters

Scott Thomas Meyers

Shall winters frost hide hearts for safekeeping?

Frozen deeply below the glassy pond

Hope ice- covered ~ Faith ever sleeping

Dreamscapes beseeching for warmth to respond

Snow swept visions of pure intimacy

Never to be chilled in the light of day

Ice flowers formed with pure intricacy

Glistening on a starry moonlit bay

Her enticing images beckon to me

Tempting me from the icy depths below

Enchantress of ice I beseech to thee

From crystalline flowers let your love show

Dreams of desire ravish the coldest heart

Winter's lust begs your passion to impart

Abstract Reality

Loves Forbidden Fruit

Subtle scents of love

Perfumed temptations abound

Lonely hearts dispute

If bliss can be truly found

In autumn's forbidden fruit

Scott Thomas Meyers

Day Dreaming

Images of you dance in my head

A cry for mercy and one for love - from God I pled.

Scarcely believing, I dared to dream of you and me.

At the moment your face I was not privy to see.

Day dreaming I dreamed of a love sound and true.

Not a typical love but a rarity shared by a privileged few.

An innocent child dreams of a love so pure.

Tender kisses - a passionate embrace that make one feel secure.

Day dreaming of a princess being rescued by her prince

Day dreams so easily forgotten sadly make my heart wince.

A pain that stabs at ones heart and shreds one soul,

These are the forgotten day dreams that once made us whole.

Day dreaming ~ again I dared to dream and to believe.

No longer would my heart allow my dreams to take leave.

Living colors now flow through my mind.

Limitations have fled and the boundaries are undefined.

Daring to believe like a child believes in a fairytale.

My mind's eye had recited for years this romantic tale.

I scarcely believed that my dreams would come true.

That is until that fateful day that I met you.

Your love is like a fairy tale dream come true.

One strong heart beats - where there were once barely two.

Day dreaming ~ two hearts and souls dreaming as one,

Has turned the over cast moon into a midnight sun.

Scott Thomas Meyers

The Starving Ninety-Nine

Moving toward an age of cooperation

Rise and fight against the greed and tyranny

We join together with one objective, rising

Voices from across the globe, crying with dignity

Lay waste to the communal intolerance

Selfishness a faded ideal from ages ago

Our freedom rest within generosity and tolerance

And revolutions begun as the narrow streets overflow

Hands humbly reaching out across borders

We stand and rise from the rod against our spines

United against the gluttonous corporate hoarders

Freedom of oppression were surrounding their shrines

We are not the materialistic one percent

We are the starving ninety nine!

Abstract Reality

Angels

I see their Garments white as snow

Their beauty radiates such that they glow

They stand and guard the huge pearl gates

As I stand in complete awe I ponder my fate

The chorus the millions sing is a beautiful melody

I stand amazed and can no longer consider my illness a tragedy

The peace that abounds envelopes around me

I then realize their angelic wings are wrapped around me

I try to look upon their beauty as I cannot see their face

Amazed I'm lost in their beauty and the fullness of their grace

My heart is deeply saddened; yes it is so

Because they now tell it's not my time to go

They bring me back here where I belong

I lay there humbled and listen to their song

Scott Thomas Meyers

Angels watching Over Me

Again I lay there and stare death in the face

However, there is a peace and love that abound in this place.

I look down; I see my body lying there

My thoughts are silenced no longer do I fear.

The hospital room is frantic; I hear the machines steady beep.

As I see myself laying there -finally at rest and in peace.

I notice first the light that fills the room

Then their wings spread out like Lilly's in full bloom.

They are gathered around me in this time and place.

I am amazed by their beauty, and the fullness of their grace.

They are translucent, yet they are full of beauty and light.

I knew then I was alone in this fight for my life.

Abstract Reality

Their beauty is unspeakable and full of glory.

I know now, with all of you I must share my story.

When they are present, hope, love, and peace abound.

Protection and encouragement, and God's Grace can be found.

No words were spoken on that eventful day.

Just a touch from the master's hand, and Gods will came into play.

Scott Thomas Meyers

The Poem of My Life

I am looking to write and leave something behind.

I dare say a legacy, something to leave my mark upon mankind.

I write with passion that comes deep from within my heart.

Something to leave behind, before this world I must depart.

It is always with passion, and hope that I fervently must write.

Hoping to touch a soul, and from my wrongs make something right.

Searching my memories deep from the past,

My heart and soul digs deep within.

Leaving my mark, and bearing my heart just so that you

don't end up where I have been.

To feel helpless when you intently look upon your life!

The hopelessness you feel when you see heartache and strife.

Abstract Reality

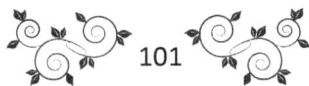

To wonder if this be my last day who would

remember and who would truly care.

Is a burden yoked to my shoulders?

So heavy that honestly with you I cannot share

I am looking for the poem of my life,

something to leave with you something that I write.

May my heart finally be set free,

and upon the wings of angels my soul take flight.

Scott Thomas Meyers

The Grandest of Plans

Spread your wings and fly amongst the eagles -

Soar to the highest of mountains to this nothing equals.

Your heart you bare not out of fear.

With complete determination you must be clear.

With the keen eyes of the bird of prey,

look for the fallen man to lift him up this very day.

Reach out pick up your fellow man.

For it is one God grandest of plans.

Abstract Reality

Is There Truly Something to Believe

I have fallen to my knees at the foot of the cross,

Feeling nothing but complete and total loss!

Words are hard to utter or even to speak.

As I kneel here sobbing at your feet.

Each drop of blood shames me as it falls.

Drop by drop your blood forever calls.

Tell me is there something here to believe.

Open my eyes and make me once again receive.

Let me feel the depths of your love.

It is the one thing I have deprived myself of.

Scott Thomas Meyers

I have fallen hard so deep and so fast.

From what I am now to what I used to be is a contrast.

I once was a tree that stood might and tall.

I was cut down and mighty was my fall.

Droplets of blood shame me as each drop falls.

However, your love and forgiveness to me your blood calls.

Let me feel the depths of your love.

It is the one thing I have deprived myself of.

I have sold myself as a slave to the highest bidder

I lay in the mud your grace and mercy are something I reconsider.

The question is can I pick myself back up.

Can I once again be overfilled with your loving cup?

Abstract Reality

I am I lost forever in this cruel and heartless world,

to which my body and soul have been completely hurled.

Tell me is there something here to believe.

Open my eyes and make me once again receive.

Is there truly something to believe in, or am I lost.

Your crucifixion was supposed to cover that cost.

Each drop of blood shames me as it falls.

Drop by drop your blood forever calls.

Scott Thomas Meyers

Frozen

I lay here lost; my feelings have become comfortably numb.

Everyone around me thinks I am going crazy;

yes this is what I have become.

I'm frozen in time as life and love passes me by.

Holding threads of hope I know I have no choice but to try.

The whispers I hear are all around.

Calling to me I try not to drown.

Cut me open and you will see that I bleed.

From a pure heart that cries out to be freed.

Is it by choice or by fate that I have become frozen?

What is the reason, I question why have I been chosen?

Abstract Reality

Is the goal to keep me from falling?

Is this my purpose, is this my calling?

To be frozen until the end of time.

Is it to speak my heart, my lyrics, and my rhyme?

To be closed off from love this can't be sane

I've tried over and over only to find out it's in vain.

I pray to thee, do I have a chance?

I lay here lost and lonely, frozen deep in this trance.

Scott Thomas Meyers

Dreams

Dreams are likened to grains of sand

Which we grasp and claw at to hold in our hands

These grains of sand, they sift through our fingers

In the end very few of our dreams seam to linger

They fall to the ground these grains of sand

Only to be trampled relentlessly upon by our fellow man

Alone in the Dark

Spinning out of control everything is just a blur

This world is ravenous with a hunger

Thirsting for a lasting emotion

Searching in an ocean of tears

Do you feel the truths of what I perceive?

The wind whispers to you

As she comes closer

Caressing you with tender care

The stars are hung with amazement

Shining in the blackness of night

Lighting your pathways

Turning your worrisome nights into day

Scott Thomas Meyers

See the sun rising from the ocean

The torch of life

Illuminating our fearful souls

Sustenance on the coldest of days

Searching forever searching

The depths of these murky waters

Praying soulfully praying

For that love that makes us whole

We are one in the same - You and I

The same desires burn in our soul

A tender touch without judging

Someone who will just show they care

Abstract Reality

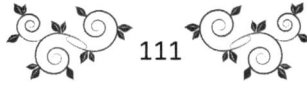

I can't be someone other than who I am

I'm already am what I was meant to be

Won't change who you are either

Just prove that you will be here

Maybe it's a mass delusion

No wonder we run scared

Look around you

Open your eyes we are all here!

Scott Thomas Meyers

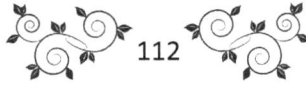

Insanity

Oh sleep dear sleep why do you escape me so

Weakened, I'm trembling, shaken to the core

Shall I forever take recess in the depths of my mind?

What madness can this be - alone in my thoughts

Deafening quiet the only noise I'm allowed to hear

Lost and wandering on celestial mystic shores

The essence of time absent of human restraints

Shackled to hope's perpetual contemplations

The verdict in - night and day a mere run on sentence!

While Sailing Upon the Open Sea

The vision of hopelessness and the totality of loss

Through the refiners fire to rid myself of the dross

Trials and tribulations were a trap from hells own fire

The plan was to shipwreck my heart and my soul to acquire

While drifting aimlessly upon this open sea

I thought myself lost - yet I was truly free

Free to dream and free to believe

Daring to dream - the colors of the universe interweave

The beauty is like none other - that nightly western sky

In the richness of these colors our hopes and dreams lie

It is there, while sailing upon the open sea

colors of the sunset blended together careless and free

The setting sun floats where the ocean meets the sky

Heartache and pain I bid my farewell and say my goodbye

Ashes to ashes and dust to dust

Into the depths of the ocean my heartaches are thrust

Scott Thomas Meyers

No More Pain

Eyes searching the breadth my heavenly home

Begging the day my true destiny will be shown

I know one day I will be completely healed

The creator's touch - truths no longer concealed

Longing nightly to be completely set free

No more pain - my one and only plea

Suffering will soon be a thing of the past

For the day will come and set me free at last

Eyes wander wayward looking to the skies above

Longing for that touch - to feel his absolute love

To rest in peace without the anguish and pain

Abstract Reality

Tribulations and trials - from these - pearls I obtain

My body broken it's only a matter of time

Meanwhile my heart spins yet another rhyme

Pain and illness have given me the song in my heart

In the midnight hours like a thief in the night

No longer will I have to lay there and fight

Scott Thomas Meyers

The Haunted

In the damp darkness of this evil night

Digging through ashes begging for one spark

Off in the distance I see a flickering light

Weary - on broken wings I take flight

Shattered mirrors reflect my empty soul

Long corridors the journeys just begun

Malicious spirits claw at my flesh and bone

An open door - my heart becomes undone

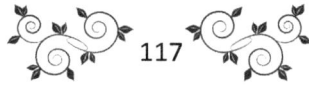

Eerie visions of loneliness heartache and shame

Taunting me from the dimly lit room

Reflecting images of the nothingness I've become

Screaming in silence there has to be something more

Feverishly knocking on all these locked doors

Haunting are the visions that await in the night

One lonely open door and a broken stairwell

A one-way expedition into the depths of hell's fire

Scott Thomas Meyers

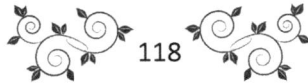

The Final Taboo – Death and Decay

Scythe clenched firmly in your skeletal hands

Busily you carve from flesh - soul away

Black-cloaked - the epitome of demise

Hourglass awaiting the last grain of sand

Ravens sing in prophetic suspicion

Eventide opens her white trumpet flowers

Hunger fills you with gangrenous desire

Hollow eyes seek out unsuspecting prey

The stale air of mystery and nuisance

Hiding fearfully from what we can't see

Menacing In the shadows of the night

While asleep we beg for the light of day

The cold kiss of sorrow eagerly waits

The final taboo – death and decay

Abstract Reality

An Unsung Melody

So many suffering broken hearts

As far as the eye can see

Running away from the agony that they feel

Fearing they have nothing left on the inside

They run and they hide

Living for the faded pale memories

Mourning the wilted flowers that have died

Haunted by shattered remains of yesterday

An army of walking wounded

Hiding in plains sight

Trembling in fear

For all the world to see

Scott Thomas Meyers

Shattered reflections of what once was

So many broken lonely people

Petrified to face tomorrow

Their head draped in indignity

Photographs and memories may fade

The rose petals may fall like dust to the earth

Sunsets will disappear into the ocean

The green grass will turn brown.

When will they open their eyes?

When will the blind see?

When will the deaf hear?

There still remains an unsung melody

Abstract Reality

Mirrors

Standing here gazing in this mirror

The aura of the nightmarish effigy

The listless glance - a counterfeit face

Continually hauntingly eyes me

Trapped within my own apathetic reflection

This hellish nightmare has stolen my soul

Eyes black as coal - catatonically glare

Penetrating the depths of the dark hollows

Trapped behind this mysterious reflective glass

A place where no living soul dares to pass

One more wretched night - am I to blame

An open door captured yet another lonely soul

Scott Thomas Meyers

Can you see what's hidden behind these glass doors?

Don't be fooled - The reflection is clear as day

Eyes sunken into the depths of their sockets

The once fleshly skin now pale and gray

Parched cracked lips hungering for thirst

Always seemingly issuing a silent cry

Is there a way of escape before I become undone?

Or Shall I sink perpetually in want and misery?

Death, abandonment, loneliness, and despair

These are the demons of the night

The monsters hiding in my closet

That shred my flesh and angrily claw at my soul

The Nether World lies just beyond the reflective pane of glass

A place where most mortals fear to pass

This is Hell – Hell – Hell!

Abstract Reality

Hopelessly trapped! This place is cold

My spirit begging from the dark shadows

Screaming my name

Fearfully shaking me to the core

Wake me - wake me!!

Running I have to escape this winding alley

These mirrors filled with black horror

The whispers in the dark calling my name

The loneliness that is driving me insane

Saving myself from this hell that I have become

Furiously smashing all the mirrors

Treading on the broken shards of glass

Finding myself where I've been helplessly trapped

Scott Thomas Meyers

Life stories

Deep within begs a story to be told

Locked up out of fear- the cork has to go

Seeping - beseeching for freedom to flow

Floodgates releasing white water rapids

With assurance the dam of fear will break

Curative rivers wash the murky banks

Through the barren valley these waters flow

These healing tales - stories of your soul

The world pleads for your accounts to be told

Abstract Reality

Winters Solace

Winters peaceful dream

Beneath the chilly night sky

Snow drifts like whip cream

Veiled hopes hide from the glass eye

Frosted dreams under stone fields

Scott Thomas Meyers

Upon a Pale Horse She Rides

Upon a pale horse she gallantly rides

Deep-dyed and wove in the fabric of time

Galloping with ease across great divides

Hooves on fire riding the celestial tides

Warnings of her coming bells strangely chime

Time ever still as the scythe briskly guides

Countless times we've met as my breath subsides

Trapped in darkened silence - turned to a mime

Probing stallion eyes watch as fate decides

Abstract Reality

Life and demise feverishly collides

Blood of black ink spilled – I'll spin you my rhyme

Desolate fields - warriors choosing sides

Fatigued from battle your passion subsides

Freed from your skeletal gasp one more time

Upon angelic wings my soul resides

From this field my painted steed takes great strides

Scott Thomas Meyers

What Stories the Heart Could Tell

What beautiful stories the heart could tell

Stolen instants gazing in subtle eyes

Two lovers enchanted under love's spell

Spilling hourglass moment's time dances by

Anticipation builds from depths within

The starry crossed gaze glazing longing eyes

Feathery traces upon begging skin

Speaking tomes of desire telling no lies

Endearing verses tenderly spoken

Pronounced from the soul taking breath away

Kisses threading lips never to be broken

Passion's expedition never to stray

Stunning adventures the soul could expel

When charming two lone hearts under its spell

Abstract Reality

Do You Dream Of Me

Time in the sandman's hand forever still

A hope rises among the restless waves

Begging answers from the tip of my quill

Hearts resurrecting from their miry graves

Imaginings in the secluded night

Standing upon this distant lonely shore

Hope carried upon angels wings take flight

Discerning myself wanting nothing more

Searching the thoughts imagined in the dark

Questions burn from infernos of the heart

Desirous want for that magical spark

From this dream-scape never shall I depart

Sprinkling fairy-tale dust to read your mind

Caretaker you're holding the precious key

What unspoken mysteries will I find?

Catcher of my dreams - do you dream of me?

Scott Thomas Meyers

Cry No More

Be still my crimson, bloodied, broken heart

No longer shall you be found weeping

Filling the oceans abysmal dark depths

Your Dreams lapping against the rocky shoals

Eternal lonely midnight hours...

Shaking frightened souls to the core

Truths beautiful revelations

Mending your broking wings to soar

Fly and be free forevermore....

Abstract Reality

About the author

Scott Thomas Meyers

Scott was born April 21 1965, in Syracuse New York, and is currently residing in New Hampshire. Writing is his way of expressing himself in hopes to reach others. Scott writes of his battle between the light and darkness as he has battled a chronic illness for the past thirteen years. His words are his legacy, his gift to give back to those who are fighting their own battles alone. Scott does not hide anything in his writings; he hides behind no masks and hopes that one day his words will affectively help others.

www.ingramcontent.com/pod-product-compliance
Lightning Source LLC
Chambersburg PA
CBHW070105070426
42448CB00038B/1721